The Determinants of India's National Military Strategy

The Determinants of India's National Military Strategy

Lieutenant General (Dr) Rakesh Sharma,
PVSM, UYSM, AVSM, VSM (Retd)

United Service Institution of India

New Delhi (India)

Vij Books India Pvt Ltd
New Delhi (India)

Published by

Vij Books India Pvt Ltd
(Publishers, Distributors & Importers)
2/19, Ansari Road
Delhi – 110 002
Phones: 91-11-43596460, 91-11-47340674
Mob: 98110 94883
e-mail: contact@vijpublishing.com
web : www.vijbooks.in

First Published in India in 2021

ISBN: 978-93-90917-15-0

Price : ₹ 295/-

Contents

Introduction

The enunciation of nations' short and long-term security strategies is inevitably based on an appraisal of the prevailing and perspective geo-strategic environment. It can be argued that in addition to domestic politics, bureaucratic politics, organisational inertia, group think, psychological barriers and learning the wrong lessons from history — failure of security strategies is also due to inappropriate assessment of the environment.[1] Therefore, in order to formulate a long-term military strategy, it is imperative to have holistic visualisation of the principal regional threats and challenges, including asymmetric ones, transnational threats, and even unanticipated ones!

The greatest challenge of our times is to be able to make correct and timely assessments of the changes taking place and the nature and extent of challenges and opportunities they present.[2] India is geographically located in a far-from-benign strategic environment, which normally argues for a strong and effective military force capable of defending territorial integrity and sovereignty from possible threats from several sources. In a democratic dispensation like India, conduct of a military campaign will always be a political decision, dictated by security considerations which are interpreted through a political lens.

Warfare has transcended beyond the three Services — Army, Navy and Air Force. New and modern domains of warfare like cyber, space, electro-magnetic spectrum and informational have emerged, most of which are in the governmental realm. More fundamentally, the notion of warfare conducted in newer operational domains, may simply not require kinetic warfare to achieve political ends. The lines between peace and war already stand subsumed or blurred. Since the domains of warfare have proliferated, multiple agencies would be equally involved in combat. Examples of these are the Central Armed Police Forces (CAPFs), National Security Council (NSC), National Technical Research Organisation (NTRO), National Cyber Security Coordinator, Defence Research & Development Organisation (DRDO), Indian Space Research Organisation (ISRO) and the Atomic Energy Commission.

Military Strategy, hence, cannot be viewed in isolation, as in the prosecution of the national security policy, the military is one instrument along with other parameters of national power — diplomacy, economic leverages, political strength and will — cumulated with soft power. It is, hence argued that in such a multi-domanial warfare environment, Joint Military Strategy must become part and parcel of the mother document, the National Military Strategy, which by itself will draw from the National Security Strategy, which would bring all elements of national power together. That brings in the necessity of both, National Defence Strategy and National Military Strategy, as exists in the U.S. In the Indian context, it is opined that the new structure of the DMA has been established seamlessly in the MOD. Creation of two separate strategies — the National Defence Strategy and National Military Strategy, will only lead to hair-splitting of thought processes and duplication within a deemed near-singular establishment!

National Military Strategy, hence, would envisage employment of all the nation's military and civil capabilities at the highest of levels and long-term planning, development and procurement to create the requisite capabilities to assure victory or success. If not enunciated by the politico-military establishment in peace, and if not planned, organised, structured, developed, trained-for or forces created in peace, then inadequacies in the achievement of political aims during war will be a national loss. Strategic history is amply populated with cases of soldiers being given impossible tasks by policymakers and of soldiers compelled to operate in the absence of clear political guidance.[3]

How do such military strategies get formulated? Indeed, it will be an exacting process. To argue further, National Military Strategy would derive itself from the political formulation of national aim, vision and interests and the National Security Strategy, implying dominant importance of political ends. India's strategic geography, which will change with time, will have clear diktats, and it would lead to a strategic context. In the oncoming era of uncertainty and increased relevance of the globally intertwined geo-strategic environment, rising challenger in China and its collusion with Pakistan, India's strategic formulations need to consider the landscape as a systemic factor. Many developments in the technological, operational, and political domains have converged to create conditions that favour the transition to discriminate force — use of military power selectively. This is attributed to the phenomenon of globalisation and the growing transparency of the battlefield. Future wars can be envisioned as being conducted with the aim of achieving a situation of political advantage and not merely victory. There is a need hence to instil a methodical constructivist rigour in the discourse for evolving determinants and consequently the creation of National Military Strategy.

This paper is accordingly laid out in six chapters as below:

- ➢ Chapter 1: Changing Strategic Geography and Geo-Strategic Context.

- ➢ Chapter 2: Strategic Threats and Challenges.

- ➢ Chapter 3: Strategic Culture and Civil-Military Relations.

- ➢ Chapter 4: Envisioning of Prospective Warfighting.

- ➢ Chapter 5: Strategic Guidance of National Security Strategy.

- ➢ Chapter 6: Formulation of National Military Strategy

The question for strategists is to first examine the formulation of the National Military Strategy from changing flashpoints of strategic geography that will draw India with an unavoidable gravity. The truth of strategic geography creates the strategic context that is the basis of National Military Strategy.

Chapter 1

The Changing Strategic Geography and Geo-Strategic Context

The South Asian Geography

The strategic geography of India is important as it relates to study of spatial areas of South Asia region as a whole and affects national security and prosperity of India. The critical aspect of strategic geography is that it changes with human needs, development of nations and their geo-political ambitions and strategic relations between them. In the context of South Asia there have been significant changes that have happened and are projected to change in the not too distant a future. South Asia comprises of Afghanistan, Bangladesh, Bhutan, India, the Maldives, Nepal, Pakistan, and Sri Lanka, covering about 4,480,000 km² or 10 per cent of the Asian landmass. South Asia has a near superpower neighbour in the North, the Peoples Republic of China (PRC).

India's geographical reality is framed by the Himalayas, the Pamir Knot, the Karakorams and the Hindu Kush to the north and northwest, the Thar desert to the West and the mountainous jungles of North East India and Myanmar. The Indian Peninsula is flanked by the Arabian Sea to the west and southwest, by the Bay of Bengal to the east and southeast, as it extends south into the IOR. Indian subcontinental ties with Afghanistan, Central and West Asia, Africa and South-East Asia are based upon contiguous historicity and culture.

The Arabian Sea borders Pakistan to the West and the Persian Gulf opens into it. The Bay of Bengal borders Bangladesh and Myanmar to the east and has the Andaman and Nicobar Islands at the mouth of the Malacca Straits.

The population of South Asia is nearly 1.9 billion or about one-fourth of the world's population, making it both, the most populous and the most densely populated geographical region in the world. Hinduism, Islam, and Buddhism are the top three religions of South Asia. Within it, there is large Muslim population and large followers of various other religions as well. Pakistan and Iran are both Islamic Republics, albeit of differing faiths, Sunni, and Shia. Bangladesh is a Muslim country. India shares a border with Myanmar which follows Buddhist traditions. In addition, Sikhism is a major religion in the Punjab region.

The Transition of Strategic Geography

Geography matters immensely and affects the South Asian region strategically. The strategic geography of the region is undergoing intense strategic transition due to the Chinese Belt and Road Initiative (BRI) and the geo-strategy of Indo-Pacific. These are certain trends that must be accepted as inevitable. The national policies of the sovereign countries of the South Asian region and the transition that these policies have led to the socio-economic developmental processes and have placed the nations in starkly differing states. *South Asia has experienced a long period of robust economic growth, averaging 6 per cent a year over the past 20 years. The region is, however, likely to experience its worst economic performance in the last 40 years, with contractions in all eight countries due to the Covid-19 pandemic. According to the latest Global Economic Prospects, the GDP in the region is projected to contract by 2.7 per cent in 2020. The Covid-19 pandemic mitigation measures will hinder internal consumption, external trade and services activity and private investment.

The Infrastructural Transformation: Belt & Road Initiative (BRI)

The BRI is the most significant engine of China's geopolitical ambitions, and South Asia is at the heart of it. While Covid-19 has moderated the BRI, it has not put it on the backburner. In the coming decade, several projects will fructify, though some may get jettisoned for various reasons. The geographic barrier of the Himalayas between Nepal and China, and Pakistan and China will be changed by railways, roads, and tunnels. China will push its technology and deep pockets to ensure that this infrastructure development will make the South Asian Nations dependent on it for a long period.

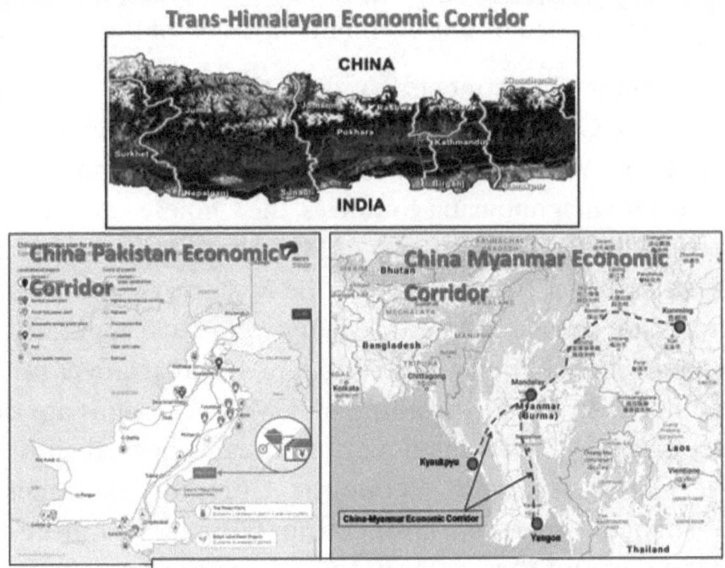

Changing Strategic Geography

It has often been stated that BRI's flagship project the China-Pakistan Economic Corridor (CPEC), may collapse under its own weight due to issues in Baluchistan, financing difficulties (especially the dire straits Pakistan's economy is in currently), the ecological fragility of the region, especially Gilgit Baltistan (G.B.), serious vagaries of terrain, altitude and weather and the geological apprehension of earthquakes/floods/landslides. Yet, because of the enormous advantages for China — geo-politically, economically and in prospecting in resources — the plan should succeed in some measure. If that happens, the entire Pakistan Occupied Kashmir (POK) and G.B. will be inundated with Chinese managers, supervisors, and workers (many of them ex-PLA). Indeed, the Chinese workers may establish a permanent presence by constructing their own administrative enclaves (as in Gwadar). The age-old socio-cultural character of G.B. will be largely subsumed in this economic invasion of the area.

China's investments under the China Myanmar Economic Corridor (CMEC) are part of China's geopolitical ambitions. With respect to the Rohingya crisis and refugee influx into neighbouring countries, the Chinese have literally become the largest supporter of Myanmar. In contrast to the Western world, China supports the Myanmar government's efforts to protect domestic stability and its approach to resolving the Rohingya issue. Though Myanmar Government had not been too forthcoming on CMEC, the signs are that the Chinese Government will eventually have their way. The China Myanmar Economic Corridor envisages a "Y-shaped" corridor connecting China's Kunming to Mandalay and then extending east and west respectively to Yangon and Kyaukpyu. These Trans-Himalayan Economic Corridors will come into being, linking Nepal and Myanmar with China's Yunnan, Sichuan and Gansu

Provinces and Tibet and Pakistan with Xinjiang and Tibet. This will allow intensive trade and interaction. Apparently, a new architecture is on the make. As part of BRI, China has been building or upgrading ports all around India — in Kyaukpyu, Burma; Chittagong, Bangladesh; Hambantota, Sri Lanka; and Gwadar, Pakistan, and in many other countries in the Indian Ocean Rim. In all these countries, China is providing substantial military and economic aid and political support.

The Geo-Strategy of Indo-Pacific

The Indo-Pacific has increasingly become a major geostrategic focal point. An approximate area of 73,556,000 sq kms, the Indian Ocean has the most critical sea lanes and choke points connecting Middle East, South and East Asia and Africa with Europe. The Indian Ocean is vital for securing movement of crude oil from the Persian Gulf and the large maritime trade within and through the Ocean. This economic and trade transit needs to be viewed within the context of the numerous, serious on-going security challenges in the Indian Ocean Region (IOR). It is no surprise that the major naval powers and regional navies have placed the Indian Ocean as a priority theatre in current and future operations, strategic planning and maritime security operations, which include counter-terrorist, counter-trafficking, and counter-piracy missions. All major powers, such as the United States, Australia, Japan, United Kingdom, France, India, and China have sought stakes in the security of the IOR. The Indian Ocean, which lies at the crossroads of Africa, Asia, and Australia, houses several littorals that play critical roles in the region.

The lexicon "Indo-Pacific" has found its way into official documents such as national security strategies, defence white papers, foreign policy, maritime security strategy and other official documents. Indo-Pacific is the multipolar region with the geographical coverage of several countries in the IOR and the Pacific Ocean. Indo-Pacific includes 43 countries from Southeast Asia, South Asia, Africa, Pacific, Middle East, Latin and North Americas and two European countries (U.K. and France). The region has emerged as an important geostrategic and geo-economic concept, gaining significance in the field of defence and security. It is a crucial space in shaping regional dynamics and the larger security architecture especially in the case of new and emerging powers. The Indo-Pacific region contributes more than half of the world's GDP and population and has huge natural resources and potential for new economic opportunities.[4] Indo-Pacific countries sharing a maritime border with the IOR or the Pacific Ocean have objectives to deepen their strategic bonding by enhancing maritime connectivity through quality infrastructure. Though these strategies or initiatives might appear to be common goals of Indo-Pacific, however, there are some differences in approaches towards Indo-Pacific construct that calls for convergence in the areas of cooperation to achieve peace and security in the Indo-Pacific region.[5]

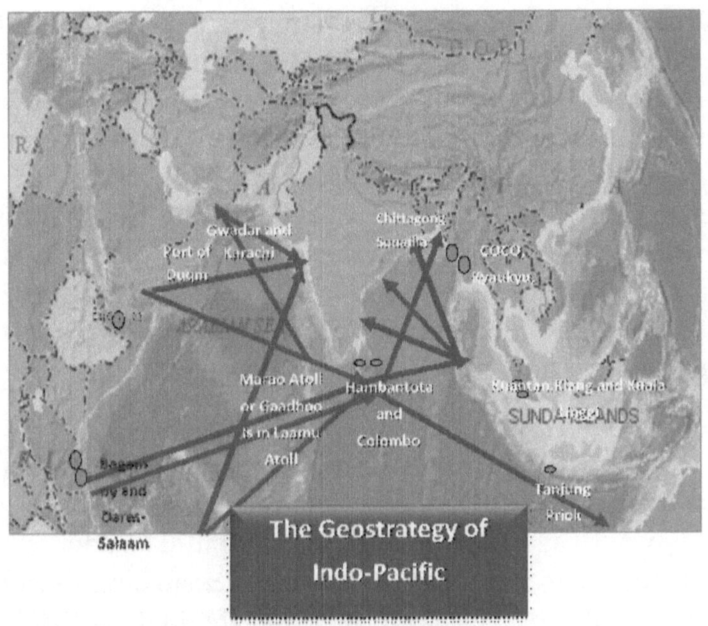

This has also coincided with the remarkable rise of China, unprecedented historically by its sheer scale and ambition. It's territorial claims in the South China Sea, its belligerence in the East China Sea and its rapid advance into the IOR through ambitious, strategic and economic initiatives like BRI, has destabilised the established international rules-based system which respected the oceans as the common heritage of mankind.[6] Militarily, Indo-Pacific is full of flashpoints as potential sources of armed conflicts. In addition, the maritime disputes and continuous violations by China, its nine-dash line in the South China Sea and the East China Sea, aggressive posture and violations are heightening the tension. The rise of China and its ambition to establish hegemony in Asia directly challenges the primacy of the U.S.

Hence, the Indo-Pacific is becoming an arena for great power competition between the U.S. and China as a new geographic space that has brought together the Indian and the Pacific Oceans; a new strategic geographic reality. For India, in its wake, it brings immense opportunities to leverage partnerships and create collaborations with Australia, France, Japan, and the United States. There are also new geopolitical challenges and strategic dilemmas, threats and challenges. There are increasing collaborations between China and Maldives, Mauritius, Seychelles, and Sri Lanka. Trade interdependence, seamless connectivity of the maritime domain affects the changing nature of the transnational maritime threat to movement of trade and energy.

India in all measures of contemplation, dominates the subcontinent, and has the biggest role in the Arabian Sea, the Bay of Bengal and the IOR. India's central location in the IOR, and in proximity to the sea lanes emanating from the Persian Gulf, the Malacca Straits and the Red Sea/ Gulf of Aden, makes it the natural naval power. Indian diaspora in the IOR nations also has its significant impact on strategic behaviour.

In sum, the changes in strategic context are laying down the basis for the state of strategic affairs for the future. China's push at infrastructural construction in Southern Asia has become extremely significant, in that Robert Kaplan's "flattening of Himalayas" and the "defeat of distance" is becoming truer. The strategic geography between India and China has clear diktats. The acceptance of Indo-Pacific as a single strategic construct linking the contiguous waters of the Western Pacific and IOR will shift the geostrategic centre of gravity to this region. The concept of "SAGAR" (Security and Growth for All in the Region) believes in an Indo-Pacific that is free, open and inclusive, and one that is founded upon a cooperative and collaborative rules-based order. It is also apparent that with increased economic stakes and larger maritime presence of other states, China will have to cover the

IOR with its naval presence, hence increasing the possibility of naval engagement in the region. The Indo-Pacific presents new opportunities to India's great power ambitions, India's priorities and significant investments will remain in the IOR. If India wants to be a major geopolitical player in Asia, it needs to leverage its strategic geography to her full advantage. The strategic geography and the transition it is undergoing have increased the threats and challenges to India.

Chapter 2

Strategic Threats and Challenges

A state's external security does depend on other states and is hence an international issue. Besides its own interest a state does have to take the interests of other states into account and to do otherwise is a bad strategy.[7] India by virtue of its strategic geography is placed in adversarial strategic environment, which mandates a strong and effective military force to ensure territorial integrity and sovereignty. India aspires to become a five trillion dollar economy in five years or so, with which will also come in extra-territorial responsibilities. This necessitates that she will have to quickly build up and consolidate military strength and choose options wisely in order to play the key role of regional balancer and stabilizer; marking out its geostrategic perimeter. Undeniably, India will be a leading power in the foreseeable future. However, India is a nation that has unsettled borders, rapidly militarised maritime environment and is also incessantly deployed in countering infiltration and terrorism, and left-wing extremism. The context of creation of a National Military Strategy hence has to be visionary and with far-reaching implications.

Aggressive China with a 'Dream'!

Chinese military strategy documents highlight the direction the PLA must take to be able to fight and win wars, deter potential adversaries, and secure Chinese national interests overseas. There is increased emphasis on the importance of the maritime and information domains, offensive air operations, long-distance mobility operations, long range precision guided vectors, space and cyber operations. China's sharpening of its claws rapidly from restructuring, exercising, and the concept of "informatization" figures prominently in PLA writings. Undoubtedly, China will have a modern military capable of modern war in near future.

China has nearly reached the pinnacle as a global power with global aspirations, and desires to re-obtain its primacy of previous times. Contemplating China's future course is 'an exercise in frustration.'[8] With a pending intransigent boundary dispute with China, it is mandatory for India to explore how the relationship with China will unfold. The 2020 tensions in Eastern Ladakh predict a continuity of aggression and belligerent attitude of China in pursuance of its geopolitical ambitions. At the same time goading its client and rentier state, Pakistan, to keep ratcheting up tensions in Kashmir aids these ambitions.

Indeed, with a focus on becoming a Great Power by 2050, using any and all means towards this goal is imperative for China. In President Xi Jinping's Report to the Party Congress in 2017, China as a 'strong power' or 'great power' was repeated twenty-six times. A key statement in the Nineteenth Party Congress was that 'China will continue to play the role of a responsible power'. This will be unmindful of any likelihood of internal political turmoil, economic decline or likelihood of a cold war with the U.S. China might give an impression of being a benign status quo power that largely supports multilaterism. However, its actions portray revisionism and expansionism to promote and shape an environment favourable to its ambitions. With increasing strength and global presence, stronger possibility exists of a threat manifesting from China in the mid and long term.

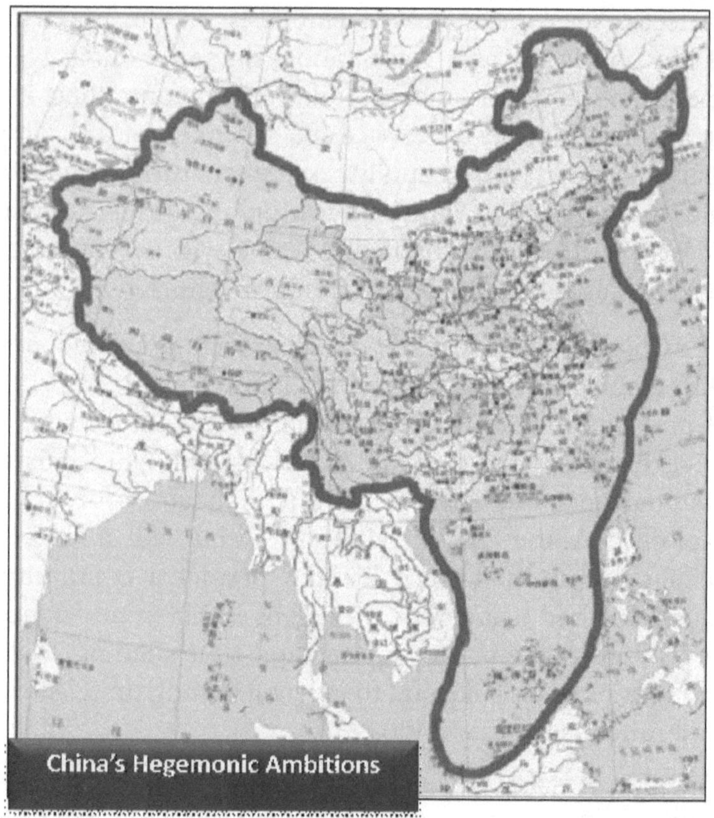

India, hence, can ill-afford to ignore China's increasing economic and military might, its assiduous strategic bases in IOR, deliberate lack of progress in the Sino-Indian border talks, and close economic and military affiliations with Pakistan. The interregnum up to 2050, with many intermediate milestones, will be an era of major tensions with India which is a major geopolitical competitor in the periphery.

Belligerence of Pakistan in Perpetuity

For Pakistan, a nation having taken birth without a clear identity, and with its inability to create and nurture one subsequently, maintaining integrity itself is an onerous task.

Pakistan suffers from a crisis of identity, and an omnipresent threat of balkanisation. Animosity with India lends Pakistan credence of identity, which is its bedrock to retaining itself as a nation-state. It is obvious that the anti-Indian-ness that is a DNA of the Pakistan Army — which virtually controls the polity of the nation — is unlikely to be done away with in the foreseeable future. Pakistan, defines its security in tangible terms — as military capability to thwart a military threat from India, and provides legitimacy to the Pakistan Army as the custodian of nationalism. The geo-strategic location of the nation, grave asymmetries in development among the provinces and the extraordinary role that the Pakistan Army has played, compounds the anxieties of Pakistan, presently, and in the future. Its current poor economic state and attempts to seek soft loans add fuel to the fire. Hence any great socio-political change in Pakistan that would lead to attitudinal change may not happen without attendant internal upheaval and instability.

It is also obvious to any discerning analyst that any comprehensive strategic transition to a more benign thinking in Pakistan in the foreseeable future is most unlikely. Pakistan would keep India embroiled in combating an intransigent Pakistan Army on the Line of Control and the International Border, and in proxy war in the hinterland. The twin pillars of the India-centric security perception are: firstly, building national military capability with the objective of challenging India's military might and secondly, providing for an effective defence, and searching for military-oriented alignments, which can assist primarily in dealing with New Delhi.[9] Pakistan therefore will remain an adversary in perpetuity, and hence does mandate hard power considerations, and a war-winning strategy.

The 'Iron' Brothers, together!

In matters of China-Pakistan collusion, Pakistan has already upgraded its security calculus with China through the CPEC. The collusive nuclear warhead-ballistic missile-military hardware nexus between China and Pakistan has grown to menacing proportions. In a similar context, despite regular interactions at the highest level, little movement is evident on the India-China Boundary question. With collusive support from China, Pakistan is also a testing ground for the latest Chinese technology, in the next conflict, or even in peacetime. It would employ a combination of different types of warfare — conventional, insurgent, terrorist, Information Warfare (I.W.) and a concoction of military and non-military, kinetic and non-kinetic. The burgeoning nexus clearly indicates a unified front of the two adversaries, in the North and the West.

The Maritime Frontier

The IOR has major SLOCs connecting Middle East/ West Asia with Europe, East Asia, Africa and the U.S., and is passage for more than 80 per cent of the world's sea-borne oil trade transits (40 per cent through Strait of Hormuz; 35 per cent through Strait of Malacca to the West Coast of USA, South East Asian nations, Japan, China, Australia), making it a lifeline of international trade and economy. It also has the world's industrial hub to its east in Asia, while to its west lies the world's largest concentration of oil reserves (80 per cent) within the Persian Gulf region. China having become the world's largest importer of raw materials and largest exporter of manufactured products, is becoming increasing assertive and is correspondingly enhancing its power, resource and market access. Through the maritime BRI, China is seeking to construct infrastructure in IOR ports to resupply and refit its naval assets. It has created port facilities in Gwadar (Pakistan), Hambantota (Sri Lanka), Chittagong (Bangladesh) and Kyakpyu (Myanmar) and Yangoon is under creation. It has established increasing Chinese maritime ties with Maldives, Seychelles and Mauritius.

China has created the world's largest and modern Navy in its attempt to expand its blue-water navy capabilities to the IOR. This all points towards Chinese intent to project power, seek to protect its maritime interests, and create a permanent naval profile in the IOR. These activities are portent of a future maritime arms race within the IOR and beyond. India in all measures of contemplation, dominates the subcontinent, and has the biggest role in the Arabian Sea, the Bay of Bengal and the IOR. India's central location in the IOR, and in proximity to the sea lanes emanating from the Persian Gulf, the Malacca Straits and the Red Sea/ Gulf of Aden, makes it the natural naval power. Indian diaspora in the IOR nations also has its significant diktats. India continues to be the dominant naval power, with vast responsibilities due to the extensive maritime trade, the island territories, vast coastline and geo-political ambitions. India has, through diplomacy, strengthened strategic links with IOR Ocean littoral states, closer ties with U.S. and its allies, and internally has built up its own military power to complement its strategic outlook. It necessitates that India continue with the build-up and modernisation programs of its maritime prowess, including amphibious, maritime air and naval, joint warfare capabilities.

Insurgencies and Terrorism

Pakistan's intransigence to support terrorist organisations and proxy war in J&K is well chronicled, as the proxy war against India gives Pakistan distinct advantages. It will remain a low cost option for it and simultaneously affects India's rise as a major power, influencing her neighbours. The

Kashmir issue being kept in public consciousness in Pakistan, allows the army to remain relevant and a sole institution of merit. Pakistan also employs technological tools like cyber warfare, information distortion, psychological warfare and propaganda, applied on nearly daily basis, while retaining a modicum of deniability. Indian Armed Forces have been and will remain committed extensively in internal security, in combating terrorism and insurgencies.

It is a truism that Indian security forces are much stronger than the irregulars in combat. The armed forces have advantages in numbers, equipment, training and discipline. However, the terrorists and insurgents — including some of the global variety like the ISIS — continue terrorism and insurgencies as it favours their distinctive strengths and cause, especially in radicalising populations and in propaganda.

Grey Zone Warfare against India

By Pakistan. In contemplating Pakistan's grey zone strategy, the relevant approach can be described as "… to reap gains, whether territorial or otherwise, that are normally associated with victory in war." [10] Pakistan without crossing established red-lines and exposing itself to the penalties and risks of escalation to conventional war, is attempting to reap success by utilizing proxies. The decade gone past has greatly enhanced the toolkit of information warfare for Pakistan from ingenuous disinformation and propaganda, to taking advantage of the social media for faster dissemination, and from fanning radicalisation to fanning civil unrests. The realm of information battlefield has provided plausible deniability to the Pakistani establishment. It is typical of Pakistan to be vigorous and aggressive in using strategic communication, and in doing so, deliberately remain well under the threshold of conventional military conflict.

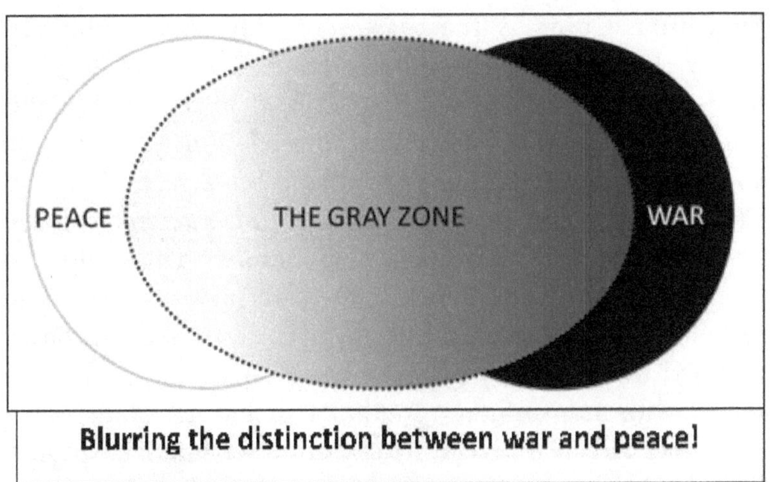

Blurring the distinction between war and peace!

The breadth of this anti-India grey zone warfare emanating from Pakistan is fairly wide, and not only related to disinformation and incitement. It remains a low-cost option in pushing in of fake Indian currency notes (FICN), drugs, hawala money, raising varied bogeys at international fora, fanning internal dissent and sponsoring terrorism by using proxies. Kashmir is but one of the manifestation of the larger geo-political rivalry of Pakistan with India. Exploiting social media using technological tools, cyber warfare, adverse information dissemination with with fakes/ deep fakes/ use of dark web and distortions is continuous, without any challenge of attributability. Cumulated with this is terrorism; Mumbai, Pathankot, Uri, Nagrota and Pulwama are a continuum. There is a very large strategic canvas created by Pakistan, to undermine Indian national security. This multi-prong offensive against India is retained below the threshold of conventional war in an ambitious grey zone campaign. India, by itself is a large and diverse nation, with a never-ending cacophony of voices and myriad problems which provide incalculable opportunities that a belligerent and adversarial Pakistan can and does easily take advantage of.

By China. China is the master of grey zone ambiguity. Henry Kissinger had opined that, *"...whereas Western tradition preferred the decisive clash of force, emphasizing feats of heroism, the Chinese ideal stressed subtlety, indirection and patient accumulation of relative advantage."*[11] Sun Tzu had centuries ago prophesized that *'all warfare is based upon deception.'* Psychological operations that would end in intellectual confusion to the adversary are part and parcel of the Chinese philosophy. 'Unrestricted Warfare'[12] nullified the boundary between battle space and non-battle space, with non-military methods including, trade wars, economic aid, resource restriction, direct financial inputs, ecological threats, network warfare and the like. The three-warfare strategy is a form of state craft that encompasses non-kinetic means to achieve political ends. The first of the three-warfares is psychological that seeks to influence and/or disrupt the opponent's decision-making capability, create doubts, foment anti-leadership sentiments and diminish the will to fight. The second, media warfare, also called public opinion warfare, is a constant on-going activity aimed at the long term influence of perceptions and attitudes, leveraging all instruments that inform and influence public opinion. And the third, legal warfare or lawfare, exploits the national and international legal system to achieve political and commercial objectives.[13] As one delves into and analyses the three-warfares, it is apparent that though military coercion may be part and parcel of the overall conceptology, political aims will be achieved largely by manipulation and economics.

In sum, the security environment of India of the future is one of concern. Hence, as geo-strategic concerns and anxieties remain, they have to be planned for. The IOR will be an arena that behoves for capabilities to stand firm even under grave provocation. Hence in the Indian context, future warfare seeks a readiness to face focused threats posed by military forces below or above the threshold of open warfare and non-military means across the full range of the threat spectrum. To be prepared for eventualities, it is understandable that future war fighting will be a national endeavour and will encompass National Power. Contextually, it is essential to delve into the strategic culture and the civil-military interface in fashioning the National Military Strategy.

Chapter 3

Strategic Culture and Civil-Military Interface

Strategic Culture: An overview

A nation state surviving without the use of force is a misconception and such a situation has never arisen in history. A nation's strategic culture determines its underlying conceptology in prosecution of wars and its distinctive style of dealing with problems of national security. Strategic culture has wide connotations. It implies the use of force or resistance to force for promoting and protecting the interest of the state and for promoting national interest by implementing a well-defined national security policy.[14] Strategic Culture is also stated as a set of shared beliefs, assumptions, and modes of behaviour, derived from common experiences and accepted narratives (both oral and written), that shape collective identity and relationships to other groups, and which determine appropriate ends and means for achieving security objectives.[15] As is apparent, strategic culture draws on and is shaped by strategic decisions and experience historically. Indeed, there is an abstract nature of strategic culture that evolves over a period of time, and can even be a tool of deception. At the ideational level, strategic culture can indicate functionality towards a particular methodology of use of force or otherwise.

Strategic culture and use of force are inseparable in most situations. Security today is no longer the responsibility of the armed forces alone. The world in the post-Cold War period has been overtaken by the information technology revolution leading towards the formation of a knowledge society. Therefore, security as a notion has become all-pervasive and needs to be defined as the complex interaction between the culture and the capability of any nation-state.[16]

Understanding an adversary's strategic culture enables one to comprehend the strategic intent. A case in point is of the Chinese Government and the CCP who tend to perceive threats of an ideological nature everywhere, biggest being from democracies. Currently, Chinese nationalism, in its basic form encompasses the pride of being Chinese, the collective memory of humiliations of the past and the aspirations for a return to greatness. Hence China's rise as an economic, political and military power has been accompanied by an outburst of nationalism among the population. Assuredly, this nationalism will make China less peaceful, more expansionist and hegemonic.

Pakistan on the other hand has developed a strategic culture which is denoted by deep-rooted belief of an existential threat from India and uses Islamic ideology to foster nationalism towards this enduring rivalry. It remains a territorially revisionist state especially on Kashmir, and openly utilises instrument of force in a proxy war to meet its ends. These perceptions are deeply entrenched in the Army, which has successfully cultivated support among Pakistan's populace.

India's Strategic Culture

"[...] is often asked, does India have a "strategic culture"? Did the trademark of the "Non-Violence" tag restrict India's strategic options? Is India inward looking and overly obsessed

with its myriad internal issues and unsavoury divisive politics of appeasement to care about long term strategic national goals and national power issues? The culture of presenting the 'other cheek' has been inhibiting in many ways. Peace at all costs has been at the cost of the country's image – making it a soft state. This affected the military mind too!![17] Of Alexander the Great's foray into India, in 327 BC, it has been stated that "*[...]there was one unexpected positive fallout, [...] gave birth to the Idea of India as a nation [...] evoke the cry of nationalism, perhaps the first time in history.*"[18] Or that "*[...]deception measures taken by (Mohammed) Ghori also played a major hand in the battle (Tarain). His letter proposing a truce lulled the Rajputs in a false sense of complacency.*"[19] Of the 1971 India Pakistan War, New York Times war correspondent wrote of the Indian Army, "*This army was something, they were great all the way, I lived with the officers and I walked with the jawans – and they were all great [...] I never saw a man flinch because he was scared.*"[20]

India's strategic culture is a complex amalgam of historic myths and legends and memories of ancient states and civilizations. The Indian subcontinent is a geographical reference, with a modern overlay of nationalism supporting a vision of Indian greatness and expectations. Deriving India's strategic culture is important for creating military strategy. And the real obstacle to the rise of India is not any more the barriers of the world, but the dogmas of Delhi.[21] "Discerning the underlying traits of India's strategic culture, its distinctiveness, and its resonance in India's contemporary actions may take some effort. But it can be done and [it is the], omniscient patrician type as opposed to others such as, theocratic, mercantilist, frontier expansionist, imperial bureaucratic, revolutionary technocratic, and marauding or predatory."[22]

India is perceived as a pacifist, having historically never invaded other territories and having borne the brunt of many invasions. Indeed strategic behaviour in dilemmatic situations could give an impression of pacifism and defensive mind-set. Even for Independence, the world recognised *Satyagraha* and civil disobedience, as the capstone of Indian struggle. It is not surprising that the defining characteristics of India's foreign policy in the first few decades after Independence were non-alignment, anti-colonialism, anti-racialism, non-violence, disarmament, and peace-making.[23] It is a factor which impacts all aspects of national security without being overtly demonstrative.[24] Indian strategic culture does conceptualise 'enemy', as an alien (organized) force whose aims or actions would deprive India of its sacred territory or subvert its society by undermining its civilized values.

Though there is a cultural influence on strategic decision making in India, it cannot be taken dogmatically that it would produce the same or similar output always. As historicity post-Independence exhibits, there may have been at times reticence and vacillation to use of force or threaten to use force. *Au contraire* often the Indian polity's decision making and execution has exhibited immense rationality and understanding of national power. The overarching opinion of pacifist India is belied by the historicity of raw courage, valour, sacrifice and stoicism in defending, Saragarhi, Rezangla and Khemkaran; and aggression and determination in offense Hajipir, 1971 East Pakistan and Kargil 1999. National strategic behaviour hence is evolving and is not resistant to change.

The larger Indian thoughts on strategy in India relate to strategic autonomy and sovereignty and nuanced approach to resolution of problems. However, territorially status-quoist strategic culture is not a given, in pursuance of operational plans. Strategic culture should drive comprehension of utilisation of National Power, and lead to joint application of armed forces. As previously operations were largely land based, the strategic culture of jointness has to be better honed. The strategic culture impacts civil military interface, which is important in evolving National Military Strategy.

Civil Military Interface and National Military Strategy

India has unsettled borders, and is incessantly deployed in countering infiltration and terrorism, and left wing extremism, and with the salience of maritime security, the bonding between the 'civil' and 'military' is imperative. "The Indian military, despite growth in its geostrategic importance, increased technological and organizational sophistication and use in internal security operations, stands firmly subordinate to civilian leaders of all parties and ideologies."[25] A strongly developing nation with profound focus on economic development and the constancy of guns versus butter debate, it is presumed that the civil-military relationship in India would have reached a kind of comfort that balances the two most imaginatively and pragmatically. For a beleaguered nation that spends $50-60 billion on defence, an assured consequence of thoughtlessly devaluing its own military will be that only second or third-rate men and women will answer the call to arms.[26]

The seven decades of relationship, had the doyen of strategic thinkers in India, Mr K. Subrahmanyam call it the "absent dialogue" that directly translated into a system where *politicians enjoy power without any responsibility, bureaucrats wield power without any accountability and the military assumes responsibility without any direction*"[27]. This well-nigh sums up in exactitude, the ways of political-bureaucratic-military equation! Indeed, the 'objective control' that Professor Samuel Huntington referred to in the seminal work, 'The Soldier and the State' focused on maximizing military effectiveness while ensuring civilian authority, and required 'the recognition (from the civilian authorities) of autonomous military professionalism'. In other words, it was to be an acknowledgement, by the civilian authorities that the military has an expertise that should not be interfered with. The politician sets the goal and the soldier is free to do what is required to achieve it, relying on his professionalism'. The issue that needs highlighting in the treatise of Prof Huntington is that 'the politician sets the goal.'

Apparently civil-military interface and national military strategy are mismatched terms in India, as far apart as it allows one to be insulated of the other. In the existential routine peacetime functioning, the bureaucracy retains a deliberate and well thought out detachment from strategy, shielding themselves from accountability and responsibility, and the political hierarchy is mired in more pressing matters and not inclined to contribute to the military's conceptualisations and war games of an unknown future.

In a democracy, like a thriving one that India is, civilian control — that is, by elected representatives of the people — is the absolute imperative. Civilian control allows a nation to base its values, institutions, and practices on the popular will rather than on the choices of military leaders, whose outlook by definition focuses on the need for internal order and external security. The military is, by necessity, among the least democratic institutions in human experience; martial customs and procedures clash by nature with individual freedom and civil liberty, the highest values in democratic societies.[28] It has been put across in distinct and pointed framework that "the principle of civilian supremacy means not only carrying out the policy directives of civilian authorities, *but also refraining from pre-empting them*. By discussing in public, questions of force or when and how to deploy it, generals can pre-empt their leaders or vitiate policy choices."[29] However, if military strategy is compounding of ideas to be implemented by military organizations to pursue desired strategic goals, then how can the strategy be formulated in a vacuum?

Civilian control over the military in India is presently addressed in multifarious ways. In matters of acquisitions and procurement, right from approval of acceptance of necessity, to in control on finances, on structuring, on promotional and human resource issues, and the like, civil control exists everywhere. On the contrary, this control that is exercised on these aspects compares most unfavourably with the involvement in matters of military strategy. While rightly accepting the competence of the Services on operational issues, the avoidance in setting of strategic goals and vision for the military creates a strange void.

On the involvement of politicians in military issues, it is has been stated that, 'the Indian politician, in spite of his strident emphasis on the principle of civil control, keeps his distance from the military and delegates the responsibility for security related matters to civil servants or technocrats.'[30] Again on similar lines, 'the Indian politician is intuitively aware that there are serious flaws in the national security structure, but political survival remains his first priority. His comfort level with the bureaucrat being high, he is happy to leave the management of defence and security matters in his hands.[31]

India's strategic culture "posits the defense of India as a geographical expression and Indian values as a society. It does not stipulate a general basis for Indian imperial ambitions (e.g., beyond specific territories in dispute in the Himalayan and Kashmir regions)".[32] The strategic culture as would have been gleaned by any adversary, is that the control is exercised by Government, in creation of national military strategy. However, the politico-bureaucratic involvement in the National Military Strategy must not be relegated to the time of involvement in combat. This needs to be constantly revised and updated in peace time. In this exercise the involvement of the elected representatives in formulation of military strategy in imperative. This is especially so since prognosis of modern wars of the 21st century clearly indicates utilisation of national power as one whole, and not exclusive to the armed forces.

Chapter 4

Strategic Envisioning of Prospective Warfighting

War is a historic constant. Nations invest billions of dollars in preparing the militaries for the next war. In history, strategists had forecast and laid down strategies and planned conduct of wars that did not eventually succeed. As the military strategy is built on the assumptions of the future, it can often go wrong. With dwindling defence budgets, and the veritable sprint in military technologies, nations are placed in a dilemma on enunciating futuristic military strategy and creating a future force. The easiest way out for the militaries is to remain in status quo, and hence it is oft stated that Generals have a tendency to 'fight the last war'.

Warfare has however seen phases of military strategies, contingent on prowess of adversaries or technological advancements. Many can be denoted with battles of attrition, mechanised warfare, manoeuvre warfare, strategic air bombing campaigns, air superiority, amphibious warfare and air-land battle, sea-control and sea-supremacy, to name a few.

Transition in Warfighting

Wars are broadly envisaged as armed, violent hostilities between states or insurgents. By implication wars entail some degree of confrontation using weapons and other military technology by armed forces employing military tactics and operational art within a broad military strategy. In the last 20 years, the pace of change has accelerated, largely due to the advent of new technologies that are transforming the way wars are fought, as well as the operating environment in which they take place. The Indian context is similar, especially the technological advancements in People's Liberation Army (PLA), and by implication its client state, Pakistan. War is generally taken as extreme violence, aggression, destruction, and mortality. The saying goes that best teacher of war, is war! Wars in future, however, will not be what they used to be. The world is changing rapidly, and the operating environment is becoming more contested, more lethal, and more complex. Future Wars may also have asymmetric battlefield tactics, which includes cyber, social, economic, and psychological strategies that may or may not necessarily involve physical combat or destruction or even armed forces direct involvement. Rapid military modernisation of PLA, proliferation of advance capabilities, including long range precision vectors, Information Warfare and use of Artificial Intelligence all necessitate an armed forces strategic overhaul, a complete revamp. Indeed, '…the categories of warfare are blurring and no longer fit into neat, tidy boxes.'[33]

The case in point in the transition of warfare is the PLA Rocket Force (PLARF) strategy that prophesises a range of deterrence, compellence, and coercive operations. The missions of a conventional missile strike campaign by PLARF could include launching firepower strikes against important targets in the enemy's campaign and strategic deep areas. Potential targets of such strikes in India may include command centres, communications hubs, radar stations, guided missile positions, air force and naval facilities, transport and logistical facilities, fuel depots, electrical power centres, and aircraft carrier strike groups. Chinese military writings on conventional missile campaigns stress the importance of surprise and indicate preference for pre-emptive strikes. Two emerging technologies relative to fresh non-kinetic domains — cyber and autonomous systems — demand contemplation. Non-kinetic means will act as force multipliers by shaping the environment, and lowering own will through coercion, and hedging leading to softening through exploitation of existing fault-lines.

The increased importance of precision guided munitions, space warfare, stealth fighters, strategic missiles and rockets are all indications of much increased lethality in warfare. China's new microwave weapon can disable missiles and paralyze tanks by shutting down electronic systems (even those with traditional shielding against EMP) by bombarding the target with energy pulses. This amount of directed energy interferes with and overloads electronic circuits, causing them to shut down. With the sprint of military technology and cybernetics, the offensiveness of the standoff attacks in future is more in the realm of a threat than imagination.

New-Age Warfare: Grey Zone

The 'grey-zone' in Indian context can be taken as state of being between war and peace, where adversaries aim to achieve geopolitical or territorial ends without overt military aggression and crossing the threshold of open warfare.[34] Contextually, the growing toolkit for coercion below the level of direct warfare being utilised by both China and Pakistan include information operations (like by Global Times and DGISPR), political coercion, economic coercion, cyber operations, proxy warfare, and provocation by state-controlled Forces on the LOC and LAC. The concept when postulated referred to *'tailored mix of conventional weapons, irregular tactics, terrorism and criminal behaviour'*[35] which soon got redefined to include, *'full range of military intelligence capabilities, non-conventional weapons, armaments, support units, and combat equipment available for instant employment…of regular forces or irregular insurgents, terrorists, or other non-state actors…'*[36]

From fake and deep fake news and online troll farms to terrorist financing and provocation of inimical elements, this kind of warfare often lies in the contested arena somewhere between routine statecraft and open warfare — the 'grey zone.' The grey zone can be taken as an area between war and peace, it is more than routine state craft, yet short of conventional war. Such a non-linear conflict can be where even state actors in addition to kinetic or military forces, employ non-kinetic means like cyber-attacks, politico-economic subversion, psychological warfare, and diplomatic pressure. The breadth of this warfare is limited only by imagination of the adversary. It is apparent hence that kinetic or non-kinetic (the latter will include cyber, social media operations, disruption of critical network infrastructure, dissension, subversion, criminal activities, currency manipulation, environmental warfare, and the like), will get aggregated or disaggregated as need be!

Technology - the Driver of Future Warfare and Military Strategies

Warfare has always remained evolutionary, but in last three decades, there has been a race to newer technologies. The prospective great transition in warfare can be ascribed to the newer technologies of the Information age — largely the computer and internet. Today this race for these newer technologies has become a sprint, and this sprint of technologies has been trending decisively in favour of disguised offense. The case in point is that land warfare in the future will be restrictive of large and heavy formations manoeuvring for deep thrusts in the plains and deserts. It will be an era when combat will in addition to conventional forces include militias, guerrillas, terror groups, precision weapons and information warfare.

Technology is placing warfare on a decisive threshold to transit into new modernity, and to forecast new warfighting strategies. In future wars, machines will make life-and-death engagement decisions, even without reliance on human interface. Taking the technological advancements in China as cue for futuristic study, the following aspects need taking cognizance off in formulating military strategy:

> PLA is sprinting to have robotic vehicles—many of which are autonomous— in maritime, aerial or land warfare. In future battlefields drone swarms of intelligent, autonomous and undercover machines will provide devastating effects on large, expensive and heavily manned systems. With the plethora of sensors of a very wide variety functional in the world, and increasingly increasing in coverage and intensity, warfare will get progressively difficult.

> Information warfare constitutes the foundation of the People's Liberation Army's Strategic Support Force (PLASSF) doctrine of winning what it calls informationised wars. Information warfare "relies upon networked information systems and informationised weapons, fighting on air, land, sea, space, and in the electromagnetic spectrum." In addition, artificial intelligence (A.I.) and other emerging technologies will change the way war is fought. A.I. can take myriad forms, but it essentially comprises algorithms capable of processing and learning from vast amounts of data and then taking decisions autonomously or semi-autonomously. A.I. is used in many weapons systems, in the tangible

world as well as in cyber space. Cyber warriors use A.I. to process large volumes of data to help detect attacks against critical infrastructures. The rapid advances in A.I. has enmeshed with cybersecurity, with the former being used to break through traditional cybersecurity systems.[37]

➢ The PLASSF is responsible for cyberspace and electronic warfare vital to its capabilities to fight and win wars. The PLASSF appears to integrate the PLA's information warfare capabilities, enabling the coordinated pursuit of electronic countermeasures, cyber-attack and defence, and psychological warfare missions. C4ISR capabilities will enable the PLA to effectively conduct joint operations and successfully prosecute "system vs system" warfare, which is essential to winning modern wars. China is attempting to utilize A.I. to direct high technology weapons capabilities, especially in cyber and E.W. domains, and leveraging Big Data and Machine Learning for 'cognitive E.W.'.

➢ The oncoming fifth generation (5G) of mobile technologies have potential military applications for autonomous vehicles, command and control (C2), intelligence, surveillance and reconnaissance (ISR) systems—which would each benefit from improved data rates and lower latency (time delay). While each of these applications could increase military effectiveness, there are concerns over data security, particularly passing sensitive information like intelligence or operational requirements over commercial systems.[38]

➢ A serious oncoming trend is Lethal Autonomous Weapon Systems (LAWS) which are weapon systems that once activated can *select and engage targets without further human intervention.* These weapons will be able to search for, decide to engage, and engage targets on their own. Beyond a point it may be impossible to abort an 'engage' decision. China argues that lethal autonomous weapons are characterized by:

- Lethality;

- Autonomy, "which means absence of human intervention and control *during the entire process* of executing a task";

- "Impossibility for termination" such that "once started there is *no way* to terminate the device";

- "Indiscriminate effect," in that it will "execute the task of killing and maiming *regardless of conditions, scenarios and targets*"; and

- "Evolution," "through interaction with the environment the device can learn autonomously, expand its functions and capabilities *in a way exceeding human expectations*" (emphasis added throughout).[39]

➤ The increased importance of precision guided munitions, space warfare, stealth fighters, strategic missiles, and rockets are all indications of much increased lethality in warfare. There is a movement towards future wars with extreme lethality. Loitering munitions, also known as lethal miniature aerial munitions (LMAMs), are a form of unmanned aircraft system that incorporate a warhead and can be thought of functionally as an unmanned kamikaze plane. Given their plane-like attributes, LMAMs can stay aloft for extended periods — thus "loitering" over a target area.[40] These are kind of loitering munitions, cruise missile or unmanned aerial vehicles (UAV) with attached explosives. The Chinese CH-901 is 1.2m long, weighs 9kg, has a top speed of 150kmph, an operation radius of 15km and an endurance of 120 minutes, On the other hand, the WS-43 has a range of 60km, carries a warhead of 20kg and can then stay above its target for 30 minutes. China's new microwave weapon can disable missiles and paralyze tanks by shutting down electronic systems (even those with traditional shielding against EMP) by bombarding the target with energy pulses between 300 and 300,000 megahertz. This amount of directed energy interferes with and overloads electronic circuits, causing them to shut down.

➢ The more that militaries rely on the electromagnetic spectrum for communications and sensing targets, the more vital it will be to win the invisible electronic war of jamming, spoofing, and deception fought through the electromagnetic spectrum. In future wars between advanced militaries, communications in contested environments is by no means assured.

➢ China is also focusing on the delivery of precision strike munitions via individual projectiles (such as cruise and ballistic missiles) rather than the platform-based strike forces (such as aircraft, ships, and submarines). Growing throughout this transformation, the Chinese missile force now consists of about 100,000 personnel.

➢ China currently fields about 1,200 conventionally armed short-range ballistic missiles (SRBMs, 300-1000 km range), 200 to 300 conventional medium-range ballistic missiles (MRBMs, 1000 to 3000 km), an indeterminate number of conventional intermediate-range ballistic missiles (IRBMs, 3000-5,500 km), and 200-300 ground launched cruise missiles (GLCMs, 1500+ km).   An initial wave of ballistic missiles would neutralize air defenses and command centres and crater the runways of military air bases, trapping aircraft on the ground. These initial paralyzing ballistic missile salvos could then be followed by waves of cruise missiles and aircraft targeting hardened aircraft shelters, aircraft parked in the open, and fuel handling and maintenance facilities. China's military is developing powerful lasers and electromagnetic railguns for use in a future "light war" involving space-based attacks on satellites.

➢ Satellites face increasing threats, starting with killer debris in the vast supersonic junkyards circling the earth. Satellites are also vulnerable to a wide array of intentional threats, such as killer satellites. "New threats to commercial and military uses of space are emerging, while increasing digital connectivity of all aspects of life, business, government, and military creates significant vulnerabilities. During conflict, attacks against our critical defense, government, and economic infrastructure must be anticipated."[41] China's has a burgeoning space program, including developing space launch vehicles, satellites, and related items. China has proven its kinetic physical counterspace capabilities several times with a range of direct-ascent ASAT systems and conventional midcourse missile interceptors that could potentially be used as an ASAT. In a conflict, China also could be capable of striking an adversary's satellite ground stations with ballistic missiles, cruise missiles, or long-range strike aircraft.   China can also pose a threat to space systems through its ability to attack the ground stations that control them with conventional forces.

➢ China's military is developing powerful lasers and electromagnetic railguns for use in a future "light war" involving space-based attacks on satellites. In 2018, the U.S. Director of National Intelligence stated that China is making advances in directed-energy technology that can "blind or damage sensitive space-based optical sensors, such as those used for remote sensing or missile defense. In 2019, there was a similar claim, stating "China likely is pursuing laser weapons to disrupt, degrade, or damage satellites and their sensors and possibly already has a limited capability to employ laser systems against satellite sensors."

➢ China has highly advanced cyber capabilities, a majority of which are run by the SSF in conjunction with its counterspace operations. Cyber contributes to the blurring of the distinction between peace and war by creating uncertainty as to what constitutes conflict in cyberspace and, in turn, the kinds of response that is appropriate. Even the question of whether a cyber-attack constitutes an 'armed attack' is pivotal. The ambit of information warfare and artificial intelligence is ever expanding with digital storage, computation, and transmission of data bits combined with miniaturization of land, air, surface, and subsurface platforms of ever-increasing mobility and endurance. Chinese hacks against secure government networks to steal personal information and technical data are well known, but the country's efforts to attack and infiltrate space systems have received relatively less attention. Additionally, recent activities demonstrate that China is proliferating its electronic and cyber capabilities.[42]

The truth is that the ongoing revolution in military technology especially in PLA demands a revolution in strategical thinking. China's leaders continue to emphasize developing a military that can fight and win. China's Military Strategy is to build strong, combat-effective armed forces capable of winning regional conflicts and employing integrated, real-time command and control networks. The PLA Air Force is shifting towards offensive operations, the PLA Ground Force's long-distance mobility operations, and the need for superiority in the information domain, including through space and lastly cyber operations. The role of non-military means of achieving political and strategic goals has grown, and in many cases they have exceeded the power of force of weapons and their effectiveness. This implies that wars in future may remain unannounced in non-kinetic format and may even be successful in achieving political goals without transcending to force-on-force wars. This amending paradigm of prospective warfare dictates fundamental changes in Indian National Military Strategy.

Chapter 5

Strategic Guidance of National Security Strategy

A traditional understanding, often attributed to Max Weber, implied that the security of states was related to threat of any change that might threaten that monopoly of nation on violence—whether through external invasion or internal rebellion. Post cessation of the Cold War, the securitisation debate broadened the concept of security. The U.N. Development Programme in 1994 came up with a report on the subject:

> *The concept of security has far too long interpreted narrowly: as security of territory from external aggression... Forgotten were legitimate concerns of ordinary people who sought security in their daily lives ...For many of them, security symbolised protection from the threat of disease, hunger, unemployment, crime, social conflict, political repression and environmental hazards.*[43]

Managing the Expansive Realm of National Security

The concept of National Security has been evolving over the years. In today's changed and complex world, security now has a much broader construct with geopolitical interests, internal stability, economic and social security, sustainability and human security. In most cases these overlap and are interlinked with the growth and well-being of its peoples. The difference between traditional and non-traditional security threats is not so water-tight now as it appeared in the last century. The conventional view of national security is that it is concerned with the preservation of state sovereignty, threats to the unity and territorial integrity, most especially its monopoly on use of force in the protection of national interests.

Hence, national security is a multifaceted and all-encompassing concept related to building comprehensive national power. It envisages a symbiotic relationship between internal and external security, reinforcing the premise that a country's external security posture is organically linked to its internal strength. External challenges can be met by effective diplomacy and adequate defence capability. To argue further, military strategy hence derives itself from a political formulation of national aim, vision and interests, implying dominant importance of political ends. It is apparent that the national security objectives, policy and strategy would be the bedrock that leads on to the development of a military strategy. Though National Security Strategy has not been formally enunciated in India, it has been deliberated in the Joint Doctrine for Indian Armed Forces.[44]

India does not, yet, have a well-articulated National Security Strategy Document, for which two reasons can be adduced. These are:

> ➢ First, there is no political consensus in the country on national security issues. For example, there is no consensus on how to treat challenges from Pakistan and China. There is little agreement on how to deal with Maoism. Similarly, the views of political parties on Kashmir and insurgencies in the North-East differ widely. Even today there is no clarity on how

the government will deal with such (Mumbai terror attacks) in the future.

➤ Secondly, the government has not been able to address the crucial issue of coordination required to formulate and address the issues of national security. The National Security Council lacks the power to enforce anything. There is no common understanding of what constitutes national security.[45]

India's National Security Strategy should establish the national long-term objectives, action programmes and resource allocation priorities, and envisage, development and coordination of all national power instruments, to achieve national goals in an ever-changing globalised environment. In the past, security strategy has often focused on external threats, and more specifically external military threats (which therefore require a military response). As has been evident over some time, it is imperative to accept that what can be regarded as developmental or policy issue, can become a major security challenge, especially of the non-traditional kind.

Hence, contextually, being a singular component of hard power, military power applies force, threatens to do so or becomes an instrument for deterring war. Military strategy would be based on futuristic scenarios, taking off from national security strategy that cumulates utilisation of national power holistically, and should last for a considerable period. The military strategy hence should not be viewed in isolation, as in prosecution of national security policy; military is an instrument along with other parameters of national power — diplomacy, economic leverages, political strength and will, cumulated with soft power.

Distilling a VISION

Preparing a National Security Strategy is an onerous responsibility as it would necessitate resilience to withstand temporary setbacks and changes. It all would commence with a well conceptualized VISION, distilled from a basket of disparate ideas and imagination, articulated with a large-picture orientation of an immediate, mid-term and distant future. The vision should be in sufficient detail to summarize the strategic objectives and intentions, be conceptual in accepting the complexity of the future, and yet encompass the thrust of military-technology and the structures imperative to achieve it. The enunciated vision should be potent enough to stir imagination to build consensus internally and create imperatives to shape the political environment by effective communication. Creating the VISION itself will be an intensive process that would require a broad-based intellectual debate, where points of view are impressed upon and substantiated or negated. Subsequently they should be reasoned, and conclusions drawn.

The ideal course hence would be initiating processes for evolving the vision through the challenges of ambiguity, navigating through this challenge by drawing on the examples of the leading global powers assuming that those are the state of the art strategies, and extrapolate these to own realities. The two imperative baskets of future military strategy and future military technology should then be followed by restructuring to implement the two, and not vice versa. The current strategies are outliving their utility, in an era where nuclear weapons are spoken off as weapons of conventional warfare by the Western adversary; where the definition of war itself is contentious — with no-contact, proxy, undeclared, hybrid, being all typologies of war; and where regimes have changed or been critically undermined by information warfare alone in its varied manifestations.

Strategic history is amply populated with cases of soldiers being given impossible tasks by policymakers and of soldiers compelled to operate in the absence of clear political guidance.[46] While formalised National Security Strategy is not available, enough pronouncements, even in the Parliament provide some direction.

Chapter 6

Formulation of National Military Strategy

The conceptualisation argued in previous chapters denotes creation of National Military Strategy with sufficient forethought and analysis, and not on a trigger. This is essential to achieve the ends, with the means at hand or likely to be available, in ways or concepts of employment as strategised. Paraphrasing it, national military strategy becomes a plan that signifies utilisation of means and concepts of employment of national power and the military, to achieve political ends. If prevention of war is the reigning theme of national power, then it must be proven by enunciation of national military strategy and concepts, creating requisite capabilities to operationalise the concepts and to train or exercise in a composite manner to attain the military aims — which would have been gleaned from political ends. The cherry on the cake is the perceptible political (and national) will and commitment to order execution of the military plans. The latter is also part of a psychological mind game. In this formulation, it is apparent that political dynamism is part and parcel of the national security apparatus and peace time planning process for evolving the military strategy. Any cleavage in this is bound to be evident by the hesitancy in committal of military power when need be, or in stipulating grave restrictions that would shackle the military in optimal utilisation of its power.

Evolution of National Military Strategy

Politics creates war, so success or failure in war is ultimately the responsibility of the political leadership.[47] War fighting strategies would have reasonable failure rate or achieve less than the end state if not envisaged with in-depth analysis. Thus, military strategy in operational execution is a military responsibility, and stating the end-state is a political task. Clausewitz insisted that politicians must understand the military instrument that they intend to use, but in historical practice that has been an exceptional condition, not the norm.[48] The duty of military leaders is to see that political leaders do not fail because they had poor advice. Hence, evolution of military strategy is two-way traffic between the Government and the military professionals, in which, in a democratic dispensation like ours, the final call will rest with the Government. Hence, the Government and the military together have to be accountable to the populace on the success or otherwise of the military strategy.

Even as a repetition, India is in a dire neighbourhood, with an active border with Pakistan, and an un-demarcated one with China, which has come alive and tense in 2020. It is unfortunate that even after four full-fledged wars, one border war and a plethora of counter-insurgency operations, where the armed forces have distinguished themselves with their valour and sacrifices, India has been unable to evolve comprehensive strategies for optimally using the military and other components of national power.[49] The IOR portents an arena that behoves for capabilities to stand firm even under grave provocation. Notwithstanding the standing affirmation of 'short intense wars', even assurance of conventional deterrence against traditional adversaries demands a military strategy blessed by the Government.

National Military Strategy envisages employment of all of a nation's military capabilities and capacities to undertake operations in domains like cyber, space and electronic warfare, at the highest of levels and long-term planning, development and procurement to assure victory or success. More fundamentally, the notion of only a military operational domain simply will not survive contact with the reality of future wars as highlighted in Chapter 4. Contextually hence the question arises whether the doctrines enunciated by the three Services in India and the joint services one, have been prepared conjoined with the Government and have the Governments' stamp of approval. *Au contraire* doctrines do not focus on 'ends' and are basically written concepts, sans physical outcomes which is the domain of strategies. The three Services have distinct separate cultures, ideals, organisations, and capabilities. The Services also tend to enhance their own tools and solutions and develop doctrines that promote their own respective interests.

Making of a military strategy is a complex bureaucratic process involving bureaucracies and intellectuals, both civilian and military. Invariably, the civilian bureaucracy considers the military as too rigid, hawkish, a little too offensive minded and with unrealistic plans. The Services obviously have not adjusted their philosophies in accordance with the political vision. One can train for the mastery of operational and tactical skills, but the imagination needed for this strategy cannot reliably be taught. All decisions for war and peace, which is akin to undeclared war, are a leap in the dark, which has to mean that even detailed analysis and honest judgements could well turn out to be wrong. National Military Strategy is however an imperative, as it would lead to creating of joint strategies, joint force structures and organisations, and a conjoined plan to create the requisite capability.

As part of the National Military Strategy, there is a joint military strategy that envisages utilisation of military force denoted by the three services, jointly.

Joint Military Strategy

Almost all conflicts that India has fought have been essentially land wars in which the Army has been the predominant player. The threats faced by the country have been focused across the border. Insurgency and low-intensity conflict have also been in its domain. The Army's size itself creates a feeling of self-importance and as a consequence, a defensive mind-set in the others. The Air Force, traditionally seen only as a supporting arm, has consistently sought an independent stature, partly by refusing to get conjoined with the others, principally the Army, and partly by stressing the strategic role of air power. The Indian Navy has a more fortunate position, operating as it does in a domain in which others can play only supporting roles. Finally, the Armed Forces, themselves, are quite happy with the existing arrangements in which each Chief operates and develops his own service almost autonomously without any involvement with the others. The political leadership has found it expedient not to disturb this unsatisfactory broth.[50]

Response to jointmanship is an attribute of underlying attitudes and to appreciate the reasons for opposition to jointmanship, it is essential to identify attitudinal traits of the military leadership. The Services guard their turf with fierce fanaticism. Every proposal that affects a Service's span of command faces strident resistance. The Services want jointmanship but with an assurance of protection of their domain, whereas jointness has to result in a reduction of the domain of each service to prevent duplication/triplication. Admiral J.G. Nadkarni frankly admits: "The Army is 20 times the size of the Indian Navy and 10 times the size of the Air Force. The first priority of the Air Force and Navy and their Chiefs in India is to maintain their identities." He further acknowledged that the two smaller Services were wary of too much jointmanship lest they and their achievements got swallowed up by the bigger Service.[51]

What then is joint military strategy? In ancient Greece, it was the "art of the general." In the USA, it is defined as the art and science of employing the armed forces of a nation to secure the objectives of national policy by the application of force, or the threat of force.[52] As stated earlier, Joint military strategy is a subset of the National Military Strategy. It can also been defined as consisting of joint objectives, ways and means, as an equation: Strategy = Ends + Ways + Means, broadly:

- Ends - Objectives that the three services strives for, gleaned from NSS

- Ways - Joint courses of action to attain the objectives

- Means- Optimal use of instruments by which ends can be achieved

The terminology of jointmanship or jointness has been constantly spoken off in the Armed Forces. Jointmanship means conducting integrated military operations with a common strategy, methodology and conduct. A country is said to have attained jointmanship of its armed forces, if it institutionalises the following:

- Joint planning, development of doctrine and policy-making.

- Joint operational commands and staff structures.

- Evolution of joint equipment policy and procurement organization.

> ➤ Integrated preparation of budget and monitoring of expenditure — both capital and revenue.

> ➤ Joint training.[53]

Joint Military Strategy consists of the establishment of military objectives, the formulation of military strategic concepts to accomplish the objectives, and the creation and use of military resources to implement the concepts. It is also imperative to mention that the 'ends' as contemplated by the political hierarchy will need translation to military 'end state' — both of which will be different. Joint military strategy hence becomes part of the National Military Strategy that would signify integrated utilisation of military means and concepts of employment of military. If achieving deterrence, credible, punitive or dissuasive, is the national strategy, then it has to be proven by enunciation of joint military concepts, creating requisite military capabilities to operationalise them and to train or exercise in a composite manner to attain the military aims.

In India, the enunciation of a joint military strategy is singularly problematic due to the sheer cleavages that exist with the polity, especially what it desires of the military in the eventuality of war or in internal situations, and without the mother National Security and Military Strategies. Inter-service issues too abound in formulation of one. As an example, the cold start/proactive strategy articulated post 26/11 terrorist attack on Indian Parliament and Operation Parakram on 2002, was an Army-specific one, as the other two services had their reservations. Military conventional deterrence remains fixated on all-out or limited high end conventional war that remains within the ambit of state versus state warfare, largely due to our contested land borders. In the case of India, conventional military superiority with the threat of deterrence by punishment is insufficient. Certain significant issues in the formulation of joint military strategy for India are as below:

> In joint military strategy the ultimate objectives are those of the national strategy. While conventional wars may be passé or limited, the military hierarchy must involve the polity at the highest of levels – to obtain guidance and directions.

> Some may say that it is unwise, impossible, or even dangerous to enunciate openly a joint military strategy. However, enunciation formally denotes arrival of India in international stage as a nation in league with others who do so. Military strategy may however, be fully or partially declaratory and/or classified or even deceptional.

> Joint Military Strategy must be 'joint' in all its forms. It should be a cumulative utilisation of national power. It will be subsequently necessary to translate it into Service-specific concepts and plans, at the

strategic and operational levels. In the operational level it is all the more important that that all corresponding tri-services echelons must operate with full synchronization.

➢ Long-range strategies must be based on estimates of future threats, objectives, and requirements, and are therefore not constrained or dominated in considerations by current force posture. Military objectives and military strategic concepts of a joint military strategy establish requirements for capabilities essential for the three Services, individually, and as a whole. The acquisition of these capabilities is in turn influenced by the availability of resources such as the annual budgets and predictive allocations. We have to consider resources as an element of joint military strategy, to avoid strategical-capabilities mismatch for the future. A case in point is the requirement of existing fourteen Corps and additional strike corps for the Army, 42 squadrons for the Air Force and 200-ship Navy (including the third aircraft carrier), with only finite resources, and each Service planning independent deterrence or concepts for winning wars. That is why operational strategies must be based on joint capabilities, and not on threats alone, as threats are examined by each Service autonomously.

➢ India will need more than one military strategy at a time. For instance, against known adversaries conventionally, combating insurgencies and terrorism, information warfare and cyber security, utilisation of Special Forces, nuclear war, as a net security provider in the region, and the like. Military strategy can change rapidly and frequently, since objectives can change or due to shifting precepts of warfare. 2020 is a pointer to a rethink on China from the objectives and policy level and downwards. A duly empowered tri-service standing organisation (including academics and veterans) contemplating Doctrines, Strategies and Concepts is imperative in this fast-changing world.

> '...Transition of India is an expression of self-confidence; its foreign policy dimension is to aspire to be a leading power... India engages the world with greater confidence and assurance'.[54] If we have aspirations, and deservedly so, we cannot avoid making seemingly awkward strategic choices. As a leading power, and if India is at the Global High Table[55] we must reappraise the current strategical framework. Only then, the standing of the Nation and the Armed Forces, will enhance credibly, and we will militarily too engage the world and the neighbours with greater confidence and assurance.

Strategising for India – Building Capabilities

"In theory, foreign policy determines military strategy... Reality is rarely so simple."[56] However, India has ventured into newer territory by moving ahead on Quadrilateral Security Dialogue (QUAD), with the US, Japan and Australia. Without entering into a formalised alliance system, the QUAD itself is a significant step forward, one that is looked upon with great consternation by our adversaries. With the agreements signed with the US over the last few years, a different message is being conveyed by India, one that will have the future of warfare and deterrence in South Asia.

A QUAD Naval Exercise in the Indian Ocean

Indian adversaries have mastered creation of an adverse narrative and use of advanced technology to embrace newer forms of warfare. It must hence be expected that in future, the conflicts that India will have to face (or is facing even currently), will necessarily and largely be with adversaries utilising psychological, economic, political, and cyber realms, in addition to contestation on the borders. Increased confusion and disorder will ensue when weaponised information abetted externally against India, would create insecurities in the populace. Conventional Indian concepts of war have to become compatible with the realities of warfare of the twenty-first century.

India hence must develop a framework of strategic deterrence against weaponised information, finance, cyber and other subversive forms of aggression — against adversaries. A 'one size fits all' national security policy would not be effective. While salience and preparations for a modern conventional and kinetic war cannot put on back-burner, accepting that a type of grey zone campaign against India may be ongoing, is critical. Hence enunciation of a

National Military Strategy followed by joint multi-domain specialisation would indicate right preparation for future warfare. That is the responsibility on the shoulders of today's political and military leaders. Seven key postulations for National Military Strategy are proffered:

➢ Non-kinetic warfare describes domains that can well be termed as largely non-military. Hence the prosecution of non-military domain aggressive actions by an adversary would cause damage or destruction to national infrastructure or socio-economic foundations of the nation. India must take such externally abetted actions as acts of war—even if the adversary is unidentifiable, un-provable or resorts to plausible deniability. Cyber contributes to the blurring of the distinction between peace and war. Even the question of whether a cyber-attack constitutes an 'armed attack' is pivotal. Cases in point would be cyber-attack on national infrastructure, power grid, banking system, and the like. War, hence may be a permanence state and must not be imagined as a territorial contest. India needs to redefine war, as even manifestations of warfare in non-military domain would hurt the foundations of the nation.

➢ Apparently, many such warfighting methodologies will not be in the exclusive military domain. Defensive and law enforcement capabilities in India symbolized by NSG, NTRO, National Cyber Coordinator, intelligence agencies, Central Armed Police Forces and State Police require parallel developments, which need to be skilfully fused in a specifically tailored National Security Structure, and be part of National Security and Military Strategies. A National Counter Terrorism Centre (NCTC) which has been on the anvil for some time, is a necessity, linked with the

National Intelligence Grid (NATGRID), and other law-enforcement and intelligence agencies. Such warfare necessitates intensive consolidation of all resources and security assets available with various infrastructural agencies, without resorting to any battle of the turf. India, with its large challenges is a right arena for an apex Internal Security organisation which has requisite data bases and analysis mechanisms.

➢ If war is the continuation of politics "by other means," (Clausewitz), social networks tend to continue politics by additional means, to influence susceptible people. As has been seen in India, this creates new, dangerous predicaments that mandate preparations. Indoctrination or causing cleavages in the society by social networks is not cyber-warfare (which uses the internet to attack and disrupt networks). A multi-pronged and concerted effort is necessary to this ever-expanding stream of diatribe. We need much better public-private cooperation and ensure that social networks establish permanent monitoring systems. There ought to be legal incentives and punitive actions for social media networks for compliance.

➢ Psychological warfare, fake news campaigns, propaganda, subversion, intimidation, demoralisation and the like, affect the Military campaigns as well. State and non-state actors are weaponising information, to the advantage of adversaries. It is not that psychological warfare and propaganda is a new realm, however the media (including social media) have multiplied manifold, its techniques are being made sophisticated, and the effect it is having on the populace is credible. Psychological warfare is leading to increasing radicalization and needs to be addressed at the earliest by parallel streams of well-planned counter-radicalisation and information management plans. Narrative Warfare and influence operations are other realms that India needs to venture into, to generate long term narratives for the nation. We also require countering adverse narratives by adversaries — a continuous stream of adverse propaganda — by focused plans. For this there is need of conjoined team of experts like social psychologists and media/ social media experts.

➤ India is a diverse and developing nation and an aspirational society that is prone to internal protestations. There is need to build sentiment analysis system to continually analyse societal anxieties. *This sentiment analysis should be a process of extracting opinions within the nation that have different schisms* — positive, negative, or neutral. With the help of sentiment analysis, we will be able to collate a nature of opinion that is reflected in documents, websites, social media feed, etc. Sentiment analysis thence can be used to monitor and analyse social phenomena, for spotting of potentially dangerous situations and determining the general mood of the society.

➤ The likelihood of strong conventional kinetic response to a hybrid non-kinetic attack or protracted grey zone campaign must not be negated. The quid pro quo response to any form of grey zone operations may emanate in a totally different realm. The issue created by the hybridisation of threats opens new vistas in deterrence debate and response options and mandates further analysis. Suffice it to say that strong conventional force will be inadequate deterrent against grey zone warfare. Hence proportional or disproportionate response cannot be predictable and will be contingent on national will and political intent at that juncture. India will require an effective bouquet of quid pro quo hybrid options, a quiver full of variable arrows that can be selectively employed, as stronger deterrence.

> The challenges of strategic cyber weaponry with adversary's malware embedded browser hacking or hardware trojans that export data unfettered, or are sleepers that can be activated on call, are dangerous portends for national infrastructure. Such cyber challenges are growing exponentially. In critical infrastructure, equipment and software must be sanitized and detection systems planned for existing systems to thwart inimical designs against the nation, or we may face as is often termed Cyber Pearl-Harbour! India has the potential internally to establish expertise for an effective defensive cyber defence, and this must be undertaken on war-footing.

The conflict and tension in civil–military relations are neatly captured in a pair of rival maxims: first, 'war is too important to be left to the generals'; and second, 'war is too important to be left to the politicians'.[57] It is argued that the status quo must not continue. In the last 20 years, the pace of change has accelerated, due in no small part, to the advent of new technologies that are transforming the way conflicts are fought, as well as the operating environment in which they take place. The pace of information warfare domain and space, and technologies like the drone-swarms, artificial intelligence, high powered microwave, autonomous systems and robotics, to name but a few, is so rapid that the doctrinal and strategic changes are unable to keep pace. Though it is easier to gloss or under-rate the changes that are in the neighbouring basements or on the near horizon, and bask in the glory of prevailing strategies, this can be detrimental for the future. The intense focus on counterinsurgency tends to relegate the likelihood of conventional operations to clichés — short, limited, localized, intense, and the like.

Conclusion

In sum, there are momentous changes afoot in the realms of warfare. Sir John Chipman heading the IISS had once famously stated that "...the world in the 20th Century lived tactically but in the 21st Century the world will have to live strategically". Obviously then, this 21st century security visualization and technological environment is leading to the challenge of crafting visions and devising optimal strategies to assist in translating our 'audacious dreams and ideas' into reality. The warfare of the future may well target civilian infrastructure by even non-kinetic means, with the adversary relying on plausible deniability. The nation will demand reprisals, without even clarity on the adversary having employed covert non-kinetic means. Traditional domains of force-on-force would co-exist in contested borders, though may have reduced salience. Technologies like cyberspace, electromagnetic spectrum and electronic warfare has expanded the domain of warfare to arena unheard of a couple of decades or so earlier. Similar expansion of information warfare, precision weaponry and autonomous systems and many more will continue to expand to newer vistas. Indeed, the Northern neighbour refers to information domination, 'winning informationised local war' and application of information technology in all aspects of war and defining military doctrine in terms of technology. It is obvious that the measure of victory in future wars will be successful paralysis rather than destruction!

The 21st century warfare hence is metamorphosing without a distinct pattern, where conventional war with increasing utilization of Special Forces, irregular war and terrorism are not dissimilar, or with fundamentally different approaches. There is an increasing blurring of distinctions between war and peace, between the different domains of conflict (land, maritime, air, space, cyber) and between kinetic and non-kinetic effect. Cyber contributes to this blurring of the distinction between peace and war by creating uncertainty as to what constitutes conflict in cyberspace. They are multiple means of war employed in combination by the adversary and conducted by both state and non-state actors. Therefore, hybridity in warfare has evolved as a combination of more than two elements of power or components of the widely spread spectrum of conflict – both kinetic and non-kinetic. Kinetic in this consideration would imply a spectrum from space weapons, CBRN, land, air, naval forces as also insurgents and terrorists. Non-kinetic would encompass diplomacy, political activities, information warfare (IW) including social media, cyber disruption of critical infrastructure, subversion, criminal and economic activities and such like conflictual activities. This evolved hybrid warfare can hence be examined as a combination of both kinetic and non-kinetic tools, used disaggregated or aggregated as and when need be!

The conflict and tension in civil–military relations are neatly captured in a pair of rival maxims: first, 'war is too important to be left to the generals'; and second, 'war is too important to be left to the politicians'.[58] Civil-military interface in India has focused too heavily on one side of the problem — how to ensure civilian control over the armed forces, while neglecting the other — how to build and field an effective military force. This imbalance in civil-military relations has caused military modernization and reforms to suffer from a lack of political guidance, disunity of purpose and effort and material and intellectual corruption.[59]

The Indian Armed Forces are one of the most significant custodians of national security. It is hence relevant to examine the official position on the principle of use of force. After the military strategy has been enunciated, and 'while the operational directive is laid down by the political leadership, the actual planning of operations is left to the armed forces and in future, the theatre commanders under the Chief of Defence Staff. Over the years, a convention has been established that in purely operational matters such advice of the armed forces is almost automatically accepted. However, in crystallizing thoughts and plans on future wars, time may not be on our side and India might already be the testing ground for military technologies, without even being aware of it. Indian Armed Forces in concert with the elements of national power need to work to eliminate the strategic and operational uncertainty, and step on the pedal. If the oncoming era is of back-end warfare — combat by programming computers, launching missiles, or operating drone swarms ensconced thousands of miles away, in safe environments, then so be it! Assuredly, warfare has a future, the all-important question is the typology of warfare, and what it would take to accept it as inevitable, and assiduously work to acquire the capabilities. The strategic conclusion is that technology has fundamentally transformed the character of war, and maybe its nature too, in a significant measure!

Indeed, the making of a National Military Strategy cannot be taken in a casual file-pushing routine exercise between the bureaucracies both at civil and military level. The systems created must envisage creation of database, constant acquisition of intelligence, to standardize the process of making strategy, and the follow-up. Over 65 billion dollars cannot be spent on defence by a developing nation, which also has serious internal and external security concerns, without a formalised military security strategy. The complexities of the strategic environment and the envisioning of future wars demand it; there are extremely high stakes in it. Or the current plans and the end state envisioned and trained for in isolation by the Services, may not find favour of the political hierarchy and dilution at that juncture may be severely detrimental. The civil-military relations as a routine functioning of the services are vital for the nation and the military.

In sum, hence, clean drafting pads and a clutch of thought leaders — military and civilian alike, and afresh contemplation of utilisation of military power optimally, and strategising 21st century war-fighting concepts, is imperative, to then plan the capabilities that would abide by us till the mid-century. National Military Strategy must be both practical and purposeful. The war-fighting strategical transition must precede any force restructuring. A *ways* transition will assuredly lead to serious well analysed credible rightsizing and internally generate substantial *means* to create a 21st century modern, forward-looking force, capable of achieving the *ends*. Such a military war-fighting philosophy will also denote that we have 'arrived', as a modern forward-looking force, with 21st century credentials.

Endnotes

1   Tang Shiping, A Systemic Theory of the Security Environment. *The Journal of Strategic Studies*, Vol 27, No 1, March 2004, pp. 1.

2   Jasjit Singh, " A Security Strategy for the 21st Century" , in AVM Kapil Kak, Ed, *Comprehensive Security for an Emerging India*, (New Delhi, Centre for Air Power Studies, 2010), p1.

3   Colin S Gray, *War, Peace and International Relations, An Introduction to Strategic History*, Rutledge, Oxon, 2007, p7

4   Prabir De and Durairaj Kumarasamy, "Emerging Perspectives of Indo-Pacific Initiatives", *RIS*, New Delhi, accessed at http://aic.ris.org.in/others/files/pdf/AICCommentary%20No%209%20September_2020.pdf

5   Ibid

6   Huma Siddiqui, "India's concept of Indo-Pacific is inclusive and across oceans", November 08, 2019 accessed at mea.gov.in/articles-in-indian-media.htm?dtl/32015/Indias_concept_of_IndoPacific_is_inclusive_and _across _oceans

7   Ibid Note1, pp 21.

8   Harvey Nelson, "The Future of Chinese State", in *The Modern Chinese State* ed. David Shanbaugh (Cambridge, UK: Cambridge University Press, 2000), p216

9   Ayesha Siddiqa, "Pakistan's Security Perspective: Problems of Linearity", in PR Kumarswamy, (ed,) Security Beyond Survival (Sage Publications, New Delhi, 2003), pp169

10 Hal Brands, 'Paradoxes of the Grey Zone, Foreign Policy Research Institute, 05 Feb 2016, accessed at https://www.fpri.org/article/2016/02/paradoxes-grey-zone/ on 29 Dec 2019

11 Henry Kissinger, *On China*, Penguin Books Ltd, London, 2012, p47.

12 Qiao Liang and Wang Xiangsui, *Unrestricted warfare*, Beijing,1999, accessed at https://www.cryptome.org/ cuw.htm

13 Stephan Halper (ed), China: The Three Warfare, Washington, DC, Office of Net Assessment, Office of the Secretary of Defense, 2013, p12.

14 Gautam Sen, "Developing Strategic Culture Role of Institutes of Higher Education and Think Tanks", Manekshaw Paper No. 53, 2014, *Centre for Land Warfare Studies, New Delhi*, accessed at https://www.claws.in/static/MP53_Developing-Strategic-Culture-Role-Of-Institutes-Of-Higher-Education-And-Think-Tanks.pdf

15 Rodney Jones, "India's Strategic Culture", *United States of America, Defense Threat Reduction Agency Advanced Systems and Concepts Office*, 31 Oct 2006, accessed at https://fas.org/irp/agency/dod/dtra/india.pdf

16 Ibid Note11

17 JS Bajwa, "Is India Finally Emerging: From its Strategic Reticence", *Indian Defence Review*, Issue Vol. 35.4 Oct-Dec 2020, 07 Dec 2020, accessed at http://www.indiandefencereview.com/news/is-india-finally-emerging-from-its-strategic-reticence/

18 Ajay and Monisha Singh, The Battles that Shaped Indian History, Pentagon Press, New Delhi, 2012, p21

19 Ibid p42

20 Ibid p285

21 S Jaishankar, *The Indian Way, Strategies for an Uncertain World*, Harper Collins Publishers, New Delhi, 2020

22 Rahul Bhonsle, "Jointness: An Indian Strategic Culture Perspective", IDSA, *Journal of Defence Studies*, Volume 1 No. 1 New Delhi, 2007, accessed at https://idsa.in/system/files/JDS1%281%292007_0.pdf

23 Rajiv Sikri, "India's Foreign Policy - Determinants, Issues and Challenge"s, Central University of Rajasthan, Ajmer February 13, 2017 accessed at https://www.mea.gov.in/distinguished-lectures-detail.htm?632

24 Ibid

25 Harsh V. Pant, 'India's Nuclear Doctrine and Command Structure: Implications for Civil-Military Relations in India', *Armed Forces and Society* 33(2), January 2007, p. 243; Paul Staniland, 'Explaining Civil-Military Relations in Complex Political Environments: India and Pakistan in Comparative Perspective', *Security Studies* 17(2), April 2008, p. 323.

26 Arun Prakash Admiral, "The Changing Civil-Military Dynamic Doesn't Serve India's Strategic Interests", in *The Wire* dated 26 Nov 2016, accessed at https://thewire.in/82627/civil-military-armed-forces/

27 Shekhar Dutt, THE CONUNDRUM OF INDIAN DEFENCE AND CIVIL-MILITARY RELATIONSHIP, in Vinod Misra (ed) Core Concerns in the Indian Defence and the Imperatives for Reforms, IDSA, Pentagon Press, New Delhi 2015, p13

28 Richard H Kohn, in Sarkesian, Sam C. "Military Professionalism and Civil-Military Relations in the West." *International Political Science Review / Revue Internationale De Science Politique*, vol. 2, no. 3, 1981, pp. 283–297.

29 NS Sisodia, "Words can also hurt" *Indian Express* on 09 Jul 2010, accessed at http://archive.indianexpress.com/news/words-can-also-hurt-me/644223/0 on 22 Jun 2017.

30 Ibid Note19 p34

31 Arun Prakash, "Roots Of Civil-Military Schism In India: The Need For Synergy, in Vinod Misra (ed) Core Concerns in the Indian Defence and the Imperatives for Reforms, IDSA, Pentagon Press, New Delhi 2015, p34

32 Rodney. W. Jones, "India's Strategic Culture", Defense Threat Reduction Agency Advanced Systems and Concepts Office, 31 Oct 2006. Accessed Dec 21, 2020 from https://fas.org/irp/agency/dod/dtra/india.pdf

33 Robert M Gates, 'A Balanced Strategy Reprogramming the Pentagon for a New Age', *Foreign Affairs*, Jan-Feb 2009.

34 Michael Green, Cathleen Hicks, Jack Cooper, "Countering Maritime Coercion in Asia", *Centre for Strategic and International Studies*, Jan 2017, https://csis-prod.s3.amazonaws.com/s3fspublic/ publication/ 170505_GreenM_CounteringCoercionAsia_Web.pdf? OnoJXfWb4A5gw

35 Frank Hoffman, Conflict in the 21st century: The Rise of Hybrid Wars, Arlington, VA, Potomac Institute for Policy Studies, 2007.

36 Max Boot, Hybrid War: A New Paradigm for Stability Operations in Failing States, Carlisle Barracks, Carlisle, PA, US Army War College, 2007.

37   Debasis Dash, Autonomy and Artificial Intelligence: The Future Ingredient of Area Denial Strategy in Land Warfare, Centre for Land Warfare Studies, New Delhi, 2018

38   PK Mallick, 5G, Huawei and India, Vivekanandan International Foundation, New Delhi, 2019, July 201

39   Elsa Kania, China's Strategic Ambiguity and Shifting Approach to Lethal Autonomous Weapons Systems, Lawfare, 17 Apr 2018, accessed at https://www.lawfareblog.com/chinas-strategic-ambiguity-and-shifting-approach-lethal-autonomous-weapons-systems

40   J Noel Williams, Killing Sanctuary: The Coming Era of Small, Smart, Pervasive Lethality, War on the Rocks, accessed at http://www.css.ethz.ch/en/services/digital-library/articles/article.html/5097848a-d36d-4918-b62c-aab6c6dee9ea on 29 Sep 2017

41   NATIONAL DEFENSE STRATEGY, UNITED STATES DEPARTMENT OF DEFENSE 2018, accessed at https://dod.defense.gov/Portals/1/Documents/pubs/2018-National-Defense-Strategy-Summary.pdf

42   TODD HARRISON, et al, Space Threat Assessment 2019 , Center for Strategic & International Studies, Washington DC, April 2019

43   *UNDP. 1994. Human Development Report 1994: New Dimensions of Human Security, available at http://www.hdr.undp.org/en/content/human-development-report-1994*

44   Indian Joint Warfare Doctrine, Directorate of Doctrine, Headquarters Integrated Defence Staff, 2017, accessed at https://ids.nic.in/IDSAdmin/upload_images/doctrine/JointDoctrineIndianArmedForces2017.p

45   Arvind Gupta, A National Security Document for India, IDSA Comment, accessed at www.idsa.in, 20 Oct 2011.

46   Colin S Gray, War, Peace and International Relations, An Introduction to Strategic History, Rutledge, Oxon, 2007, p7

47   Christopher Bassford, *POLICY, POLITICS, WAR, and MILITARY STRATEGY, Maine Corps Doctrinal Publication 1-1, Strategy, 1997, available online at http://www.clausewitz.com/readings/Bassford/StrategyDraft/*

48   Ibid Note3, p7

49   Vijay Oberoi, *Indian Defence Review*,   Issue Vol. 30.1 Jan-Mar 2015 | Date : 02 Mar , 2015

50   PS Das, NAMICS OF MODERN WARFARE, Jointness in India's Military —What it is and What it Must Be, Journal of Defence Studies, IDSA New Delhi, August 2007, Volume:1, Issue:1 accessed at https://idsa.in/jds/1_1_2007_jointnessinindiasmilitary_psdas

51   Ibid

52   JCS Pub. 1: Dictionary of Military and Associated Terms. Washington: U.S. Department of Defense, June 1, 1987, p. 232.

53   Mrinal Suman, Jointmanship And Attitudinal Issues, IDSA, *Journal of Defence Studies*, Volume 1 No. 1 New Delhi, 2007, accessed at https://idsa.in/system/files/JDS1%281%292007_0.pdf

54   Jaishankar S, IISS Fullerton Lecture at Singapore Jul 2015, accessed at timesofindia.indiatimes.com>articleshow,

55   Teresita C Schaffer and Howard B Schaffer, India at the Global high table The Quest for Regional Primacy and Strategic Autonomy, The Brookings Institution, (Harper Collins Publishers, Noida India, 2016).

56   Richard K Betts, Soldiers, Statesmen and Cold War Crises, Harward University Press, 1997

57   Ibid Note3, p7

58   Ibid Note3, p7

59   Stephen P. Cohen and Sunil Dasgupta, The Drag on India's Military Growth, Policy Brief #176 Brookings Institution, Washington DC, 2010,